I WANT THAT PENCIL

SHARPEN your CASHFLOW, PENCIL your FUTURE.

JAMES CHEN

PARTRIDGE

Copyright © 2020 by James Chen.

Library of Congress Control Number: 2020913411
ISBN: Hardcover 978-1-5437-5974-7
Softcover 978-1-5437-5972-3
eBook 978-1-5437-5973-0

All rights reserved. No part of this book may be used or reproduced by any means, graphic, electronic, or mechanical, including photocopying, recording, taping or by any information storage retrieval system without the written permission of the author except in the case of brief quotations embodied in critical articles and reviews.

Because of the dynamic nature of the Internet, any web addresses or links contained in this book may have changed since publication and may no longer be valid. The views expressed in this work are solely those of the author and do not necessarily reflect the views of the publisher, and the publisher hereby disclaims any responsibility for them.

Print information available on the last page.

To order additional copies of this book, contact
Toll Free +65 3165 7531 (Singapore)
Toll Free +60 3 3099 4412 (Malaysia)
orders.singapore@partridgepublishing.com

www.partridgepublishing.com/singapore

CONTENTS

Acknowledgements vii

Chapter 1   Why That Pencil? 1
Chapter 2   Be the CEO of Your Money 7
Chapter 3   Wealth Is Not Equal to Income 11
Chapter 4   Passive vs Active Inflow 19
Chapter 5   Up Your Wealth 31
Chapter 6   Understanding Your Money Map 39
Chapter 7   Being Honest with Your Crystal Ball 53
Chapter 8   Beyond That Pencil 57

Epilogue 59
Appendix 61

Acknowledgements

Going in the right direction in life is never easy. It is something that many struggle with, even today. Despite the amount of hard work most of us are willing to put in, our desired destination often can only be arrived at through guidance from people along the way. Fortunately, I am blessed to have met three wise mentors who were there to guide me in different stages of my life. I am where I am today because of them, and they are the reason this book came into existence.

My first mentor was Mr Peter Siong. He was a tough and charismatic man with very high standards. He expected no mistakes from his team and upheld these standards himself as well. He was very strict with tardiness of work and would reject something immediately if it was not up to his standards. He was also an excellent speaker onstage and off. He was very eloquent and would always capture the attention of the people he wanted to address. It was through him that I learnt to uphold the standards of the work I now produce. I have also become more meticulous when it comes to handling work.

My second mentor is Mr Kwek Chor Wen. He has given me a different perspective on management and taught me how to be a leader. This is the reason I am able to lead a team of more than fifteen people today. He is a very nice and people-oriented boss who cares for the well-being of the people working for him. He showed me that different people have different characters and strengths, and it is our role as leaders to bring out the best in them and get them to work together harmoniously in a group.

My third mentor is Mr Raymond Lim. Raymond is known as a man with ideas that are out of this world, and he constantly challenges me to break through my own limits. He believes in helping people to grow and that people should always challenge themselves, increasing their limits and threshold. Throughout the years, he really has inspired me to become a creative and daring individual. He is like a big brother to me and is the one who inspired me to publish the book that you are reading now.

The purpose of this book is to extend a hand and provide guidance to everyone who is facing difficulties in managing wealth. I want to do so by transferring what I've been learning all these years from my mentors, along with my knowledge of money management and moneymaking. I believe that this will help you to see the bigger picture of your cash flow and manage it accordingly, which will hopefully help you in achieving what you want in the end.

I would like to thank the people who have given me ideas and helped me in the development of this Money Map concept and the publication of this book. I couldn't have done it without them—and especially my family, who supports me in all the things I do.

1

WHY THAT PENCIL?

When I was growing up, my family was not one of the stereotypical wealthy Singaporean families you often see in the movies. In fact, I grew up in a low-income family and rarely had the luxury of owning new and trendy items. My parents were hard-working people. They worked to provide for the family and make ends meet. They worked so hard to pay the bills and buy daily necessities that they often ended up with nothing to spend on themselves.

As they were constantly working, my younger brother, Jimmy, and I grew up not spending much time with our parents; this included not having dinner together. Even so, my parents are still the greatest role models in my life, and it is them and their genes that instilled the hardworking spirit in me. I grew up knowing that I wanted to provide a better life for my children—to have dinner comfortably as a family without worrying or stressing over whether we would have enough for the next meal.

I believe in giving back to the community and helping those who are underprivileged, as I came from a household like theirs. This is the key factor behind my drive and passion to serve in the community. I find joy in helping low-income families. I want to lift some of their financial burden off their shoulders so that they can live a better life and improve their standard of living. Hence, I started a programme that provides complimentary tuition for students from underprivileged families, in the hope of blessing these children in their studies so they can grow up and provide a better life for their family.

1.1 Scholastic ambitions

I remember times when my entire family, including my grandparents, lived together in a one-bedroom flat. My grandfather was a fisherman; my grandmother was a housewife. My mother was a factory worker, and my father was a welder. I remember how busy my parents were. They would wake up very early in the morning and come home very late at night. We rarely had the chance to eat together as a family. My father would often share stories with us and would say that some of the dividers along the expressway were welded by him.

I was very proud of my father and used to share these stories with my friends. Even though my parents did not earn a lot, they always tried their best to provide for and support my younger brother and I to the best of their capabilities. I never once thought that my family was poor; yes, we might not have had a lot of money, but we were a happy family. My parents loved one another, and they loved my brother and I dearly. However, it was only after I grew up and looked back that I realised how much they loved us through their constant hard work and their desire to provide us with better food and nicer clothes.

When I turned 7, it was time for me to enter primary school. I remember my parents searching high and low, trying to find the top primary schools in our region to enrol me in. I recall their disappointment when there weren't any available spots left in that particular prestigious school, and we could only join the already-long waiting list. I ended up having to enrol in a nearby school instead.

Surprisingly, just before the school term started, the prestigious school called and informed us that we were next on the waiting list. My parents were so happy, as they had thought that enrolling their child in a prestigious school could mean the end of their poverty. Their dream was for me to study hard and get a good qualification so that I could secure a stable and good job in the civil service. I would have my whole life provided for and would not have to be in a constant state of worry over whether I could provide for and support my family like them.

1.2 THE PENCIL

When I was in primary 3 (around the age of 9), the mechanical pencil was introduced. It was a trend in school then to use mechanical pencils instead of the normal wooden pencils, and the latest model was one that could dispense lead just by shaking the pencil. I called it the shaker pencil. My tablemate would bring it to school every day to use it. He would shake the pencil every time to dispense its lead, and I would get so jealous over it.

Knowing that my parents could not afford it, and really wanting to have the pencil so badly, I actually stole it from him. When I brought that pencil home, my mother saw it and asked where I got it. Unable to lie, I confessed that I had stolen it from my tablemate.

Needless to say, she was furious; she scolded me and said many things to me that evening. One of those things stood out and stuck with me even till today: "We might be poor, but we should never steal. We want to be honest people."

I had to return the pencil to my friend the next day. It was a valuable lesson that changed everything I do. I still live by my mother's words today.

Truth is, I still do want that pencil. However, the pencil I want is no longer the one that shakes to dispense lead. It has evolved into a metal structure with four wheels and a four-storey concrete structure. The point is, no matter your age, there is always something you want, something you desire. It could be a car, a new house, a private jet, or even a new mobile phone. These are things that we desire to have—bigger and better. This is the reason I've worked so hard every day and even today. It is to get the pencils I want and wanted.

1.3 Two paths to the pencil

No matter how hard I studied, my results were nothing compared to Jimmy's. My younger brother's academics were really good—and not only was he book-smart, he was street-smart as well. Jimmy's grades were always better than mine.

Right after national service, Jimmy decided not to continue with his university education and took the entrepreneur path. He started his own business as a full-commission financial consultant. Meanwhile, I took the conservative route and joined the air force, hoping for a more stable income.

Jimmy's income grew exponentially, and by the time I was earning $3,400 a month in the air force, Jimmy was already earning more than $5,000 per month. I joined the bank right after the air force, and because I was trying to work back my lost income, I did not take a single day off during my first six months.

When I left my corporate job at the age of 37 to venture into my own wealth-management business, Jimmy's income was already 2.5 times more than mine, and he also had more control of his time. If I could do it all again, I would have definitely chosen entrepreneurship ten years ago when I left the air force.

1.4 Why I do what I do

Over the past twelve years, I have worked hard to chase after my pencils. What about you? What is your pencil today? And what are you doing to obtain your pencil?

Due to the dispute I had with my mother regarding the shaker pencil and the valuable lesson she taught me, for the longest period, it has been my principle to work hard to achieve what I want. I studied hard and worked even harder. I didn't take many breaks, and I worked even on weekends. Any time my clients or my business partners wanted to meet me, I would always be available, even late at night. I wanted to earn more so that I would be able to afford the things I want and never have to be jealous of what others had.

I also wanted to give the best to my son, Jaden. When Jaden told me that most of his classmates had an iPad, I wanted to get him an iPad as well. I didn't want him to feel jealous over what others had, like I did when I was a child. He didn't need to be the first person to own an item, but if everyone else had it, I wanted to be able to get it for him too.

I will share how I started to work in the bank later in this book, but it was there that one of my rich clients taught me another valuable lesson. He said: "Working hard doesn't necessarily work; you need to have the mindset of the rich and successful and think like they do." He challenged me to think about what he said and gave me an interesting analogy. He said that if there was a reset button today and you pressed it, resetting every single person's wealth to zero, would you become rich? It was a fair question; we couldn't claim that only the rich got richer and the poor got poorer.

Just as I was writing this book, the world was experiencing the worst virus pandemic ever. The world is now at risk of going into a recession, and this is what I told everyone: the wealth is transferring and the game is resetting. If you have the mindset of the rich, this is your opportunity to become rich.

The thing about rich and successful people is that they have the right mindset, so they will always be rich and successful while the poor will remain poor. The right mindset sets them on a different path from others. They believe they are rich even if their bank account does not reflect that. This sets them apart.

I knew from the moment I learned about it that I wanted to have the mindset of the rich. I was interested in finding out more about how they think. Working in the bank opened up opportunities for me to work with high-net-worth individuals. Slowly, I gained a better understanding of how and what they think.

Now I have started my own business, and through years of experience in entrepreneurship, I have actually combined my personal experience and all the know-how related to finance to create a concept called the Money Map. It is a simple, proven concept that will give you an overview of your finances and assist you in getting that pencil.

2

BE THE CEO OF YOUR MONEY

What is the first step you can take to become rich and get those pencils you want? Today, even if stock prices or property prices were to fall by 40 per cent, would you have enough money to buy shares or properties? Ask yourself the following questions to determine whether you are the CEO of your money:

- Do you find it hard to manage your money?
- Are you constantly in debt or running out of money?
- Do you want to increase the savings in your savings account?

Most of us don't manage our money; we are managed by it. We buy luxury items or overspend on our expenses. We incur debts through credit cards and loans. We spend future money. We end up not able to clear off our debts and incur late charges and interest. We end up working for money rather than having our money work for us. We chase the wrong things, such as seeking higher income but forgetting about managing our expenses.

2.1 Cash flow

A common misconception is that if income increases, net worth will increase as well. This is not true; there is another factor to be taken into consideration, and that's cash flow management. *Cash flow* is the inflow and outflow of cash. I am not talking about income and expenses and the balance sheet; I am talking about the flow of money. This is not taught in schools. Teachers talk about income and expenses, but what's more important is actually your cash flow. You can have big assets, but if you don't have cash flow, you will still be bankrupt.

Let me share with you how it works and why it is different than what you may have learned. Suppose you're earning $10,000 a month, and you spend $1,000 on expensive shoes. That $1,000 is an expense. More importantly, it is a cash outflow.

What if you had chosen to save that $1,000? How would that be categorized? As long as the money flowed out of your pocket, it would be identified as an outflow. Investments also represent a cash outflow. If you purchase too much insurances or too many long-term investments and your monthly cash flow is very tight, you are sacrificing current opportunities, and you will miss out on them.

This is what cash flow management is all about. It manages the inflow and outflow of cash. This is important because it gives you knowledge of exactly where your money goes. Knowing where your money goes can help you with two things:

- increasing assets and wealth
- managing liabilities and opportunities

2.2 Net worth

Once you're done managing your cash flow, you can move on to managing your net worth. In financial terms, net worth is assets minus liabilities. *Assets* are things that increase in value and give you a positive cash flow. *Liabilities* are the opposite of assets. They give you a negative cash flow, as you have to pay off your debts.

Let's take $1,000 as an example again. If $1,000 every month goes into a savings account, after twelve months, it becomes $12,000, excluding the tiny interest you earn from the bank. This $12,000 becomes an asset. If you have no loans and no liabilities, the $12,000 is added to your net worth.

2.3 Allocation

Once you've built a certain and substantiated amount of assets, you can move on to allocation. How do you allocate these assets effectively, and what do you want to achieve by allocating them? Are there pencils you want to get? My main objective is to help you build inflow to help you get the pencils you want.

I will help you generate a passive inflow for yourself. I don't call it *income*, because I want you to understand the concept of cash flow. This means that you're making these assets work hard for you so you don't have to exchange anything for them. They will generate income that goes into your cash flow and becomes a cash inflow—a positive income.

This is all done through allocation, which is similar to playing Monopoly. When you land on an empty space, you will have to decide if you want to buy it or not. In real life, allocation generally boils down to four asset classes:

- cash
- bonds
- equities
- alternative investments

Today, there are many alternative investments available in the markets, including bitcoins and properties.

How will you know where to allocate your money so that it is effective? The most important thing is to look at risks. A common mistake many people make when investing is not looking at and considering risks. With allocation, you'll be balancing your risks and allocating your money effectively so that you can earn passive inflow.

Think about it: you have worked hard for a long time, waking up at seven every morning, starting work at nine, and only knocking off work at six in the evening or later. By the time you are home, it is already eight o'clock. I highly recommend that you allocate your money effectively so that it generates passive inflow and works for you. Once you are able to generate more passive inflow than your expenses, you practically do not have to work anymore.

3

WEALTH IS NOT EQUAL TO INCOME

I can still remember clearly the day I received my last pay cheque from the air force. It included a gratuity for serving in the air force for the past six years, which amounted to about $16,000. That was the last cheque I received from them. I remember asking myself, "Is this all I'm worth, after working for the air force for six years—$16,000?" Can you imagine how lost I was?

When I left the air force, I had nothing. I didn't have an insurance plan, I didn't have an investment plan, and I had become accustomed to relying on the government and believing that the civil service would take care of me for life. I believed that they'd take care of me and my retirement, but that was far from the truth. No one owes you a living.

I recall that during my years in the air force, I wasn't very prudent in my spending. Indeed, I spent every single cent I earned. I didn't bother putting aside some money to learn new skills. When I was out, I'd always buy things I didn't really need, and I never thought to save for my retirement or for the day I'd leave the air force. I thought I'd always be working for the government. I didn't plan for an alternative and just spent my money lavishly.

I left the air force with my $16,000 pay cheque, walked into the bank, and deposited it. I still recall sitting down in a café wondering what to do next for my career. I wasn't sure what I wanted to do, but I knew that I needed to make more or at least close to what I was getting in the air force. I had been earning about $3,200 a month.

I needed a job urgently, and I didn't know what to do. I called up some of my air force seniors who had left the force. Some were working as property consultants, some as sales engineers, and some as air traffic controllers with the Civil Aviation Authority of Singapore.

None of those appealed to me. I was really lost; I didn't know what I wanted to do. All I knew was that I needed to make enough. I kept thinking that if I earned more, I would be rich. I kept browsing the net, looking at all the available job-posting websites like JobStreet and Gumtree, and one particular job stood out to me: working in a bank as a personal banker.

At that point in time, I knew neither what a personal banker was nor what the job scope might be. I went online to research and read up on the profession. I found out that personal bankers manage money, and I thought, *Since I don't understand how to manage own my money, why don't I become a personal banker? I can learn how to manage money for customers and at the same time, learn how to manage money for myself.*

With this thought in mind, I went for my first interview for a personal banker role with one of the local banks. I wasn't at all prepared, yet I still went ahead with the interview. Turned out, I couldn't get the job at all. I managed to pass the profiling test but failed at the face-to-face interview.

Still believing that this job was meant for me, I went to another foreign bank, and guess what? I couldn't get the job there either. At this point, some people might feel that the job was just a bad fit. However, with my headstrong personality, I refused to give up. In fact, I was even more determined to get the job. I always walked into bank branches and saw how personal bankers dressed in nice shirts, neckties, and coats. I saw them greeting customers and welcoming clients to the branch. I could imagine myself doing this. I wanted to earn as much as the people in the bank did, so I continued to try.

Back then, there were three local banks in Singapore. I applied at all three of the local banks and most of the foreign banks. Finally, one of the banks took me in. That marked the beginning of my career as a personal banker.

3.1 Managing wealth

My journey as a banker has taught me many things. One is how the rich manage their money. It's totally different from how most people do it, and the way they look at money is also very different.

When I first started working at the bank, I'd always compare people's wealth based on their income. If you earn $2,000 and I earn $5,000, it appears that I am at least twice as wealthy as you, but this is not necessarily true. Nobody manages wealth by looking at income. I was very wrong to have such an idea and perception of money.

The rich manage wealth by looking at their net worth. I only vaguely understood the term *net worth* at the time. I'd heard of it and learnt it in school, but I had never applied it in real life. My job in the bank gave me a totally different perspective. Someone with a monthly income of $10,000 could have a net worth of more than a million dollars.

3.2 Working hard and working smart

Another thing I learnt at the bank is that a bank isn't an easy place to work. The job was tough. I remember that during the first six months of my career, I didn't even take a single day off or take any of my annual leave. I worked seven days a week. The bank was open five and a half days, with Saturdays being the half day when it closed at two in the afternoon. For the first six months, I didn't hit my target during the weekdays, and on Saturdays when the bank branch closed, I'd travel all the way to another branch at Toa Payoh which has extended banking hours to do my duty there. I was always trying to clock in enough sales so that I could achieve my weekly targets. If I didn't, I'd even work on Sundays.

I worked every single day for the first six months of my career in order to achieve my goals. It was a painful and tiring experience, but I grew and learnt a lot from it. Despite my hard work, I saw friends getting posted to better branches, where they earned much more than me, and they did not have to work seven days a week. Life felt unfair, and I was upset over it.

I soon realised that my original philosophy, "Work hard to achieve what I want," wasn't as true and as realistic as I imagined it to be. It is not just about how *hard* you work but also how *smart* you work. For the next few months, I continued working very hard and even asked to be posted to another branch so that I could have a higher chance of hitting my targets.

At the bank, I was the quietest banker among my colleagues, and I usually didn't speak up. Whichever branch my boss or manager assigned me to, I'd just take it without question. However, after working for more than a year, I would no longer stay quiet. I was very determined to succeed. I wanted to earn more. I spoke up, requested a change of branch, and fought very hard for it.

Eventually, I was told that to move to a specific branch, I had to change my role and became a financial protection specialist focusing on risk management and insurance. I wished I had spoken up earlier. The transfer was approved, but this time around, I'd focus solely on wealth protection.

With my new role and new branch, I was given the opportunity to work with high-net-worth individuals as well as bankers, because I was attached to a relationship manager in the bank. Fortunately, the branch I was in had a high-net-worth centre beside it. This gave me a chance to deal with many high-net-worth individuals. I worked hard and did very well. I was the top insurance specialist for the whole channel. I started earning money and managed to clear off some of my credit card debt, as I was a spendthrift. Life was going well for me. I started to save for myself and for my first HDB unit.

3.3 Cash flow struggles

Years before, my parents had put me in a prestigious primary school hoping I would become a civil servant with a stable income, which I ultimately did. Working as a civil servant meant that my pay cheque was never delayed. The amount sent on the tenth of every month was prompt and accurate—not a single cent more or less. Due to this security,

I felt that my monthly salary was good enough to spend every month. I did not save any of it.

After I left the air force, cash flow became a serious problem. Within a month, I was lost. I didn't know how to manage my money. I was close to losing all the money I had, as I did not have any savings.

Over the next few years, my focus was always on chasing a pay cheque. I thought that the higher my income, the bigger my wealth would be, which of course was not true. The more income I earned, the more I spent. No matter how much I earned, I could never save up, not even for an emergency fund.

Actually, many people are like this. They run into big cash flow problems, such as not having enough emergency funds, running into debt, and spending all their money one day after collecting their pay cheques. When their income increases, so do their expenses and lifestyle. They are forever trapped in this rat race, like a hamster running on wheels, not getting anywhere but exerting a lot of effort.

To get rich, it is not about increasing your income, it is about managing your cash flow. There are many people who draw a big salary but are unable to manage their money simply because they don't know how to. Truth is, cash flow management is really simple. I will be explaining how simple cash flow is and how to manage it as well as providing examples on how it can be relatable. Managing cash flow is the first step to getting your pencil.

3.4 Mindset of the rich

Let's say I ask you how much you have in the bank right now, and your answer is, "Not much, maybe $25,000." How do you make this $25,000 work for you? How do you take this $25,000 and multiply it? Some people might reply, "If only I had more money, I could start a business. I could invest in properties. I could earn more money and get rich." The thing is, even if I gave you $1 million or more right now, you still wouldn't know what to do with the money.

The reason is simple: you have the wrong mindset. You refuse to learn how to multiply the money you have on hand, even if it's only a little. This is why my mentor said that even if everyone's net worth was reset to zero today, the rich would still end up being rich, and the poor would remain poor. The important lesson here is to never chase money or think that the only solution is having more money, because the truth is, there will never be a time when you can say, "I have enough money to get rich now."

Instead, learn to make whatever you have work for you—work in your favour. Let money chase itself into your pocket. I have spent my life doing things that I didn't even understand until a later stage of my career. I had the opportunity, or maybe I should say I created the opportunity, to help a multinational company (MNC) set up its distribution channel in Singapore. I saw from the newspaper that a Japanese MNC was venturing into Singapore, and I actually searched for the person in charge and recommended myself to him on social media. You can see how aggressive and proactive I was as a person through this example.

I really enjoyed what I was doing—getting my hands dirty through the process of setting up. I was taking care of the recruitment, training, sales process, and business. I was so excited to be putting what I had learnt all those years ago from Peter Siong into action.

Looking back, I was always being given projects to set up new channels and revamp training departments, and it was really tough to do all these. It was like setting up your own company. I got to decide the logo design and the branch design as well as the sales procedures. I felt that I was underpaid for all the work I had been doing. I was definitely worth more than that.

One day, I walked up to my Japanese CEO and asked him if I could invest and be given a share of the company. I believed in the thing I was doing and felt it would make the company profitable. I saw potential in the company. He gave me a surprised look and said that he had been working for the company for over thirty years but did not own any shares. He told me that as a pioneer staff member in the local company, I had lots of opportunities to be appointed as the CEO of a Singapore entity, and he saw great potential in me.

However, I did not want to be a CEO. I have never wanted to be a CEO. I wanted to own company shares. I had put in my hard work and sweat, and I just wanted a fair piece of the company I had helped to set up. After hearing his reply, I was more certain of my decision to leave and set up my own venture. The following day, I put in my resignation.

The following month, I started my own company with Gaius Ng and CK Seah, and from there, my journey of entrepreneurship began. The journey has been fruitful, and I wish I had taken this path earlier.

4

PASSIVE VS ACTIVE INFLOW

Many people have talked about passive income. I've heard it discussed online, by people I know, by retirees, but I never really understood what it meant. I think the best way to understand *passive* income is to first understand *active* income.

I see earning an income as a form of exchanging and providing services. If you're earning $5,000 a month, it isn't exactly earning but more of an exchange. So, what are you exchanging? To get that $5,000 every month, you're simply exchanging your time and ideas for money. Unless it is a business set up by yourself with your own ideas, most of the time these ideas are exchanged for money from your boss. This earning is called an *active income*, and you have to exchange something for it.

Passive income is the exact opposite. It is income that does not require you to exchange anything for it. You don't have to work for it. Your assets could be generating a positive cash flow for you without you doing anything.

I have a client whose mother is retired. Her father drives part-time as a taxi driver. He earns a little over $2,000 a month. Their house—two-bedroom public housing—is fully paid for and has no other liability or loans. Their investments are mainly in corporate bonds and unit trusts that create a regular stream of monthly income. These investments bring them around $2,000 every month. Their income far exceeds their monthly expenses. They have gotten out of the rat race.

My question to you is, would you consider them rich or poor? Is wealth equivalent to income? They might not be wealthy if we define it using numbers because they don't have millions of dollars. Their income might not be high, yet they have achieved true financial freedom, and they do not need to worry about their finances. If you ask them whether they feel wealthy, they will tell you that they have no money worries or financial anxiety. They are comfortable with their house, and they spend within their means.

Another dream most people have is to invest in an additional property and then collect rent from it, or to buy a bigger property, downsize, and cash out the amount as they are nearing their retirement. People prefer physical and tangible assets when it comes to investment, but they forget that the risk is high when they put all their money into one big single investment. They lose out on current opportunities when they overcommit and risk losing big when this leveraged investment goes a different way. These investment methods are profitable only if people understand how to manage their cash flow properly.

As mentioned above, overcommitting on current cash flow means you give up on current opportunities to earn money, and this is a common issue for many people. Let's say you overcommit yourself to a private apartment that is above your cash flow level. After working for many years in the same industry, you are approached by an ex-boss who suggests the two of you start a business together. You might find this to be a really good opportunity, something not to be missed. However, because of your overcommitment to your private apartment, you don't have enough in your current cash flow to take advantage of the opportunity. Thus, it is important to refrain from overcommitting yourself to anything above your cash flow level. You never know when an opportunity may suddenly arise.

Let's recap what you learnt from school: income − expenses = savings. If these savings are used to buy suitable assets, they can generate a passive income for you. If your income is higher than your expenses, you won't have to work anymore. I've seen many customers do it. The right mindset is all it takes. I hope this book will guide you into making the right choices with your savings so that you will be able to generate passive income.

4.1 Positive vs negative cash flow

To be frank, understanding your income and expenses is useless if you don't understand your cash flow; that is what you should really know. There are only two directions in which money flows: it's either coming in or going out. You have cash inflow or cash outflow. Understanding cash flow is very different from managing your expenses. The focus is different. There are two types of cash flow: positive and negative.

Let's say I receive a salary of $5,000 today. This money coming into my pocket is a positive cash flow. However, on the same day, I decide to get a $1,000 gift for a friend. This gift is a negative cash flow. After that, I want to put $500 into my savings plan. You might ask, is that considered a positive or negative cash flow, since technically it is still my money in the end? This is the part where people usually get confused, since savings is supposedly a good thing. But it is actually a negative cash flow: it is money going out of your pocket. When the savings plans have matured and the money comes back into your pocket, it will then be considered a positive cash flow.

How about going on a holiday and exchanging money for a foreign currency? Is this transaction a positive or negative cash flow? Here's the question to ask yourself: is the money still in your pocket? Since you are exchanging one currency for another, there is no real transaction, no flow of money. There is only a flow of money when you spend money. The same goes for external wallets or apps that allow e-wallets, whereby you transfer a portion of your money into another app but have not spent that amount. This is not considered cash flow, as the money is not spent, nor is it new income.

Many people have the misconception that if they buy many savings plans, it will tighten their cash flow in the future, and so they will have more money in the future. While this is true in the sense that it does help you in the future, many of these people plan and save so much for future consumption that they leave only a little for today. If you can't survive today or if you're suffering now for the sake of the future, what is the point of it?

I believe in balance so that you can have a decent amount of savings that will be beneficial for you in the future yet still enjoy your current season. That's the point of life, isn't it? To be able to enjoy life now and, of course, in the future as well.

Assume that $\$5,000 - \$1,000 - \$500 = \$3,500$ is your cash flow every month. Whatever is left behind is your savings, right? However, this amount never seems to stick around, no matter how hard you try to budget every month. This is due to something called leakages.

Before we talk about leakages, though, here is an example of an outflow of cash, tracked using a mobile application. Every wedge in the pie chart represents a specific outflow; as long as it goes out to somewhere you can't touch for the time being, it is thrown into this pie. This way of managing your cash flow allows you to see where all your expenses are at a glance.

As you can see, the majority of my outflow goes into church tithing, joint account, and food. As church and my joint account represent pretty much the same amount of cash outflow every month, my next heaviest expense would be food. If I want to budget for the next month—or if there happens to be more than one special occasion, such as weddings or birthdays, in the next month—I can see at a glance which part of my expenses must be cut down to cover those additional expenses. This is what is meant by managing cash flow.

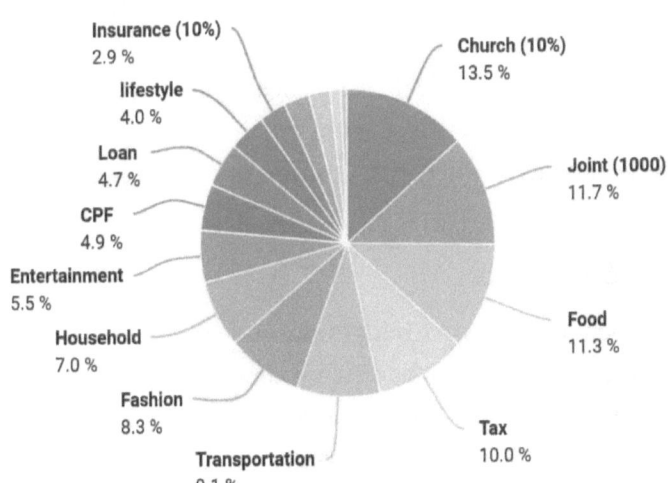

4.2 Leakages

In cash flow management, inflow − outflow = savings. Theoretically, if you are earning $5,000 and you spend $4,000, your savings should be $1,000. But by the end of the month, you seem to only have $500. Why is this so? From the net cash flow to the actual savings, there is something called *leakage*.

So, what is leakage? An example of leakage would be if you're out with friends and offer to pay for drinks. This generosity causes you to exceed your budget, spending more than you should have. Other examples include gifts for birthdays or baby showers where your friends suggest a more expensive gift, causing you to exceed your budget. It could also be a sudden change of plan where you were supposed to grab a coffee from the coffee shop for only $1 but instead went to Starbucks for a $6 drink instead.

The main point here is not to encourage you to be a stingy person but to understand the need for budgeting and allocation, which are important in the management of cash flow. This will aid in your savings when you slowly understand where the leakages are and tweak accordingly to ensure that you minimise these leaks. The leakages can be very big and swing your cash flow from positive to negative—from positive savings to a negative position to even going into debt.

4.3 60–10 Rule

When it comes to budgeting and allocation, how can you ensure that you are budgeting appropriately? I personally apply the 60–10 rule. Many of you may have heard of such rules, as often taught by Westerners, but my suggestion is the 60–10 rule, which is more applicable to the Asian context because of our culture. This is part of my Money Map concept. By the 60–10 rule, I mean 60 and 4 ´ 10 as shown in the chart below.

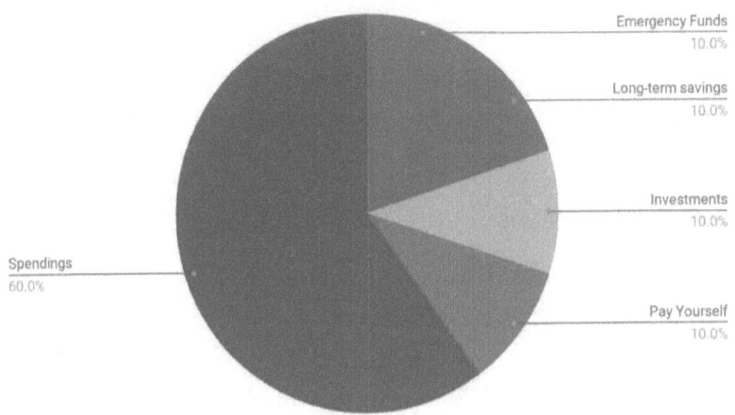

So, what do these breakdowns mean?

4.3.1 Spending (60 per cent)

My suggestion is that 60 per cent of your income should be used for spending. This amount will represent your expenses for the month. If you're a Christian and tithe monthly to a church, the 10 per cent of your monthly income should be deducted from this portion, as it is outgoing cash flow. Some people have asked me what happens if they want to buy an expensive watch; do they budget it here? My answer is yes. If you have committed yourself to an instalment plan, the cash flow basically comes from this allocation.

For the next 4 ´ 10 per cent, I would like to break it down as such: emergency funds, long-term savings, investments, and pay yourself. These will be further elaborated later on.

Simply put, the 60–10 rule helps to map out how you should allocate your money, especially when your salary comes in. If you are committing yourself to an insurance or investment plan, you will need to know how and where to allocate the cash flow. This will help provide a clear picture of how much you need and how much you can use to drive passive income and increase your savings for the future.

4.3.2 Emergency funds (first 10 per cent)

Emergency funds are savings that should be able to sustain you for three to six months if you are out of a job Assuming you earn $10,000 every month, $1,000 should be set aside for emergency funds. My recommendation for an emergency fund is around three to six months' worth of your monthly expenses, depending on your age. This is something most books or financial planners will not tell you.

So how do you gauge how much you need? Well, if you're younger, like in your twenties or thirties, the chances of finding another job is high. As your age increases, it gets tougher to look for a job, and you'd tend to be pickier as well. For example, if you were earning $10,000 per month before you lost your job, you probably would think twice about whether you wanted to take up a new job that only offers $8,000 or involves a significantly different job scope. Therefore, the older you are, the more you should allocate to your emergency funds, as it would generally take more time for you to look for another job.

Everyone needs emergency funds and should not make the same mistakes I did when I came out of the air force. I had no emergency funds and didn't know how to handle money. On the flip side, what happens if you have too much saved for an emergency? That is not good either. The money is now sitting there, not working for you, and not increasing itself for you. You've worked hard for the money, and now that money should work for you. After you've saved six months' worth of expenses as emergency funds, the rest can be considered excess. You can, and you should, use this money for investments and other savings.

4.3.3 Long-term savings (second 10 per cent)

Long-term savings, as the name suggests, should be savings for the future. It can be for retirement or for a long-term goal. Examples of a long-term goal are goals that are ten or twenty years down the road. It could be saving to get a car or a down payment for a property. Note that these savings are not something you should take out and set aside if you have no money left for the month to spend on your expenses.

So, once again, if you're earning $10,000, you should put aside $1,000 for long-term savings. I'm talking about really long-term savings, which can't be compared to emergency funds. Emergency funds are short-term, meaning you're taking a typical bank's interest rate at current board rate. With long-term savings, you must be able to stomach a little more risk. You can take on ten- to twenty-year instruments such as bonds, preference shares, or a long-term savings plan. These will generally give you an interest return according to the current market rate, which is around 2 to 4 per cent, depending on the instrument you choose to put your money into. Hence, it will help you to earn more as you save for the long term.

4.3.4 Investments (third 10 per cent)

The third 10 per cent is for investments. Unlike emergency funds, which are short-term savings, this means that when you press the ATM buttons, the money from the emergency fund must be available. Hence, emergency funds are placed in banks. At banks, the interest rate is less than 1 per cent. Today, that 10 per cent you set aside for investment can actually take on a higher risk, something you think can bring you a higher return, maybe 4 to 5 per cent more. Some of these instruments are known as unit trusts, stocks, shares, or any other instruments that can give you a better return.

You may choose to save this amount in the bank, with less than 1 per cent interest, or in a savings plan that gives you about 3 per cent. However, I don't think this is a wise decision. My suggestion is to use it to invest in something that gives you an interest rate of 5 to 8 per cent or a property investment that can give you an interest rate of 9 to 10 per cent. If you're worried about losing this money through investment, my stand is that you don't have to worry because this amount has already been budgeted and allocated. You can take the risk of investing in investment instruments with higher returns. I believe that if you can allocate your money this way, you'll be able to save quite a substantial amount of money for retirement.

4.3.5 Pay yourself (fourth 10 per cent)

The last 10 per cent is what you pay yourself. What does paying yourself mean? It means that in a month, you should set this amount aside so that you can invest back into yourself. Every day, you give your time to your company, customers, partners, and family. How often do you actually spend time for and on yourself? We often don't invest in ourselves enough, which is why 10 per cent of our income should be devoted to this.

With the economy moving at a fast pace, change has now become the constant. You should always be improving yourself by learning new skills or a new language. With the 10 per cent allocated to paying yourself, you can look for courses related to your career, but know that this amount is not to be spent on a holiday. It is for you to add value to yourself. For example, if you're an engineer, you should be looking around for any professional certificates your industry offers so that you're able to upgrade yourself. By upgrading yourself, you increase your level and value, which could potentially increase your earnings by 10 to 20 per cent or more.

If you are unhappy with what you are doing and have been wanting to try something else, such as flower arranging or photography, or if you are keen to learn a new language, take this 10 per cent and go sign up for a course. This 10 per cent is to pay yourself. Do anything with it as long as it increases your personal value. If by the end of the year, you can't seem to find a suitable course, then donate this money to a charity of your choice. Since you've already budgeted it, you can do anything you like with it.

5

UP YOUR WEALTH

Once you achieve the habit and skills of managing your budget and cashflow, you are ready to move to the next stage of wealth creation. The mistake most people make is jumping straight into asset building without first managing their budget and cashflow. If you have yet to master the concept in the earlier chapter, please read and understand it before moving on.

We start by understanding the definition of asset and liability and how to multiply it.

5.1 Multiply your assets

What are assets? As mentioned in chapter 2, *assets* are things that increase in value and give you a positive cash flow. *Liabilities* are the opposite of assets. They give you a negative cash flow, as you have to pay off your debts. To identify whether an expensive item is worth your money, ask yourself these questions: What kind of value will it give me? Will it increase in value, and will it provide a positive cash flow? If the answer to these questions is no, then this expensive item is likely not worth buying or investing in.

On your Money Map, there should be a portion where you can list all the assets you own as well as the amount they are worth. This will give you a quick view of your current assets on hand. Once all the details of your assets, liabilities, risks, and more are clear, you can see your total net worth and how to increase it. The typical asset classes are as follows:

ASSETS

-
-

Property :
Vehicle :
Cash Savings :
CPF OA :
CPF SA :
CPF MA :
Others :
Others :

Total Assets :

- cash
- bonds
- equities
- alternative, e.g. properties

Property consultants will say that a property is the best investment. However, based on an analysis from 1975 to 2017, statistics have shown that Singapore residential properties only gave a return of 6.8 per cent. Singapore's stocks and shares perform better at 7.6 per cent, and global stocks give you about 8.4 per cent.

This data doesn't mean much to Singaporeans, as property is still the most popular asset class. The reason is that properties allow us to leverage, which is a powerful tool. With a 20 per cent down payment, you are able to get a $1.2 to $1.4 million property. This means that your net worth and assets are being multiplied by five. Also, property gives you very steady capital growth, especially in Singapore, where land is scarce. It gives you a very stable growth and doubles your money.

Property is a physical asset, as I mentioned briefly in the earlier parts of this book. Physical assets are tangible. They can be seen, touched, and enjoyed, and give you an opportunity to add value as well. People tend to favour tangible assets to show off their wealth.

Taking loans is one of the ways to make it happen, and since the interest rate is relatively low now, there are good opportunities for people to invest and leverage. For example, in the past, the property interest rate was about 1.2 per cent. Now, it has increased to 1.9 per cent. Over the years, the compounded interest may start to stagger up, and you will realise you're working to pay off interest. Have you ever wondered how great it would be if there were no interest rates or if the accumulated interest rate could be less? If we could reduce the accumulated interest rate, we would save about 20 per cent more per month. You could then use that 20 per cent for something else.

Nowadays, there are also a lot of lifestyle wants. I used to train someone whose biggest pitfall, I soon realised, was his management of cash flow. Many people are now in debt, and that is why we came up with a section in the Money Map concept called *risk management*, which is also known as *debt management* if you are in debt. This section of the Money Map shows you the unmanageable debts and health risks you could potentially be exposed to due to your family history or lifestyle habits. This will assist you in your understanding of what kind of risk solutions you will need instead of getting the wrong ones or getting those that are not as needful. With the correct solutions, the remaining money could be used for something else. Instead of paying for unnecessary insurance, you could be earning money.

For example, you could be earning $5,000 a month but spend all of that $5,000 every month. Even if you tried saving $200, at the end of the month, you may end up not saving the full amount. This is due to leakages, as I've mentioned previously, and it affects the cash flow. Leakages occur due to impromptu decisions made which require extra funds, or you could have purchased too much insurance and cash flow is so tight you cannot even have a decent savings account. These are causes that affect your budget every month, and some of this unexpected spending might cause your expenses to exceed what you had planned.

5.2 Rule of 72

There is a simple rule that I'll be teaching you: the rule of 72. When you place your emergency funds in the bank, the bank will give you an interest rate of 0.05 per cent. To make calculations easier for this explanation, imagine getting a premium rate of 1 per cent from banks instead of 0.05 per cent.

With a 1 per cent compounded interest rate and $100,000, how long do you think it would take for the amount to double? I'll save you the hassle of calculation and tell you that it takes 72 years to get that $100,000 to double in your bank at 1 per cent interest.

We will use the formula $72/x$, where x represents the interest rate various instruments can get you. With this formula, you can see and compare how different interest rates can double your money. If you allocate the money into a savings plan that gives you a 3 per cent interest rate, the formula will derive to 72/3, which is 24 years. With an interest rate of 3 per cent, it will take twenty-four years to double your money. What happens if your interest rate is 5 per cent? How many years will it take for your money to double? 72/5 = 14.4 years. This is actually a typical investment plan, and some of the instruments—including bonds and unit trusts—can actually double your wealth in fourteen years. Now, what if I offer you an interest rate of 8 per cent? How long would it take to double up? 72/8 = 9 years!

To lay it out clearly, I'm basically talking about bank savings, savings plans, unit trusts, or other investments (could be property investment) to give you a clearer illustration of the different levels of interest, as you have seen.

The big question is: How would you allocate your money? It all depends on the risk you're willing to take. However, always remember, the bigger or faster the returns, the higher the risk incurred. Many people fall into the pit of greediness, investing in high-risk products before they even set aside the money for investment. They use their savings or emergency funds to invest, and this is a huge mistake we should not make.

5.3 Take charge of your liabilities

What are liabilities? Liabilities are all about debts. Examples of debts are household debts and credit card loans. According to statistics from 2004 to 2017, as assets increase, debts also increase significantly. However, these statistics don't go into detail on what kind of debts were actually owed. The highest amount of household debt is actually property, followed by car. As the years go by, personal loans and credit card loans have been increasing, especially among people in their late thirties.

LIABILITIES
-
-

Housing Loan :
Car Loan :
Study Loan :
Personal Loan :
Others:
 :
Others:
 :

Total Liabilities :

In order to get that pencil, you have to make sure you don't end up losing all of the other items in your pencil case. Another factor to remember is not to trade for the shaker pencil with something expensive you don't own—for example, a limited edition silver correction tape. If you are planning to borrow someone else's silver correction tape to pay for the shaker pencil, you best be sure that the shaker pencil is worth the price of the silver correction tape, or that it is able to get you three silver correction tapes in return. Only then should you take up this loan so that you can return the silver correction tape and have some for yourself. But this mechanical pencil will then have to work hard enough for you to get you more silver correction tapes to pay back your debts. Basically, the item you took a loan to purchase better be able to produce back at least three times the amount you borrowed for it. If not, it is not worth the loan.

As with assets, there is a small portion for liabilities under the Money Map. This provides a breakdown of all your short-term and long-term liabilities. When you have a clear breakdown, you can allocate your money properly.

5.4 Good Debt

There are two categories of debt: good and bad. If the amount borrowed increases your net worth and has a future value, then it is *good debt*. Linking back to my story on the silver correction tape, if borrowing the silver correction tape from someone else and exchanging it for the shaker pencil will get you back three silver correction tapes' worth or more, only then is it worth taking up this debt. That would be a good debt, as the end return will not only allow you to cover your loan but exceed it and benefit you financially in the future. Examples of good debts include house loans and leverage investments that buy into a share or property. If you were to take out a sum of money to buy land or plantations, these will be considered good debts and good debt management.

5.5 Bad debt

A common example of bad debt would be credit card debt. As credit card debt increases, not all of what is owed can be paid off completely. In Singapore, there are currently $5.2 billion worth of unpaid credit card debts, and this amount is actually quite high. The interest rate for credit cards ranges from 24 to 25 per cent. If the amount owed is $10,000, the amount payable will be $12,400. This interest amount of $2,400 could be used more wisely in other areas, such as investments. Then, not only would you save yourself from paying an unnecessary interest fee, you could invest this amount and get more in return.

Does it mean that we should not incur any debt? The answer is no. We need debt too, but only good debt that will help us improve our finances in the long run.

6

UNDERSTANDING YOUR MONEY MAP

In order to understand the Money Map concept effectively and to its fullest potential, it is important to know how it can actually be used and structured for people of different age groups. With the different roles and responsibilities that come with those age groups, the way to make use of this concept definitely changes along the way. In addition to knowing how to use the Money Map effectively, it is also important to be aware of the common mistakes people make when it comes to handling finances. Therefore, I will be sharing a few of those financial mistakes and explaining the different ways to utilise the Money Map for five different groups of people, which I feel make up the majority of us.

6.1 AGE GROUPS

Through the years, I've met people from all age groups. Personally, I belong to the late thirties/early forties group. I have spoken to many people around my age and found that we are actually quite similar when it comes to choice of fashion, the way we work, and the way we react to things. From those I've encountered along the way and through countless conversations, I've come to an opinionated conclusion about my own age group and others.

6.1.1 Loyal generation

The *loyal generation* refers to the group of people who are in their fifties, also known as Generation X. They are the ones who will stay in a job no matter what happens. They are loyal to their job till the very end and do not believe in changing jobs for career progression. Their bosses could reprimand them every day and they might be unhappy with the job, but they will still remain in it, simply because they are used to being inside, in their comfort zone. They are also a generation who saves a lot of money and does not spend lavishly, often fixing broken things instead of getting new ones.

6.1.2 Late thirties/early forties

Next comes the generation of people who are in their late thirties and early forties. They are a generation who are very into branded goods that are big and obvious—meaning they enjoy wearing clothing or accessories that have the brand's logo displayed for all to see. The reason they are so into branded goods is possibly due to the fact that credit cards were introduced to them during their youth. Having the idea that they can get luxurious goods first before paying was something new and enticing, so many of them actually overspent and landed themselves credit card loans if not personal loan debt.

6.1.3 Early twenties

The generation of people in their early twenties are also known as the millennials. This group of people love branded goods as well, but they prefer to be minimalistic. Their clothing and apparel can cost a lot, but the logo will be small and unobvious. A plain white T-shirt with a small branded logo printed on the left chest pocket can easily cost $300 or more, and yet they will still get it and claim that the quality of the shirt is better than others.

This younger generation of people are the ones who have not officially started to work, yet somehow they can afford to buy branded goods and travel around the world. So where does their money come from? It probably comes from their part-time jobs or from their parents (Generation X) who worked so hard to save money. The worrisome factor for this generation is that they might face some difficulties when it comes to managing money. This is the reason for the publication of this book—to help young people learn how to manage their money.

6.2 Financial mistakes in life

Entering adult life can be very intimidating for many, especially because of the responsibilities that come with adulthood and stepping into society. With all these new responsibilities and commitments, it is very common to make financial mistakes that can and should be caught and corrected as early as possible. The following are some of the most common mistakes.

6.2.1 Incurring bad debts

The most frequently incurred bad debts are credit card debts. When given a credit card, people often treat it as a ticket to buying everything they want. They disregard the high interest rate that comes along with their spending. When they overspend and can't afford to pay off their debts, they take on a loan to settle those debts. Some even sign up for a new credit card to pay off the debts of their current card. With this, they plunge into a tornado of recurring debts; with the high interest rate, the debt will start looking like it's never-ending.

So, exactly how much interest are you actually paying for credit card debt? To break it down, if you owe $10,000 worth of debts and the interest is at 25 per cent per annum, the interest you pay every year is $2,500. This is equivalent to half or all of the month's salary of a college graduate. In fact, you could've used this amount in other areas to help you to earn more money. To those who just started working, always remember that you shouldn't spend what isn't yours yet. If you have rolling credit card debts, please work to get them cleared. The rolling interest is going to make you work harder for your money.

6.2.2 Spending on lifestyle

The reason behind this financial mistake is that many people cannot manage their budgets. The sudden influx of money from their pay encourages them to spend and buy the things they had been longing to have. The thought is, "If I could survive in the past with less than $500 per month, I can definitely control my spending next time and not worry if I have to survive with little money in the future."

They fail to realise that as their income increases, their expenses will increase as well. Their needs and wants will grow, and so will the desire to live luxuriously. Many may think that as their expenses increase, they will still be able to go back to their simpler days. The truth is, it is not as easy to revert back to your old lifestyle as you imagine. If one day you lose your job, if you have debts and your emergency funds are not prepared, it will be a disaster.

6.2.3 BALANCE BETWEEN RISK AND RETURN

Young people are generally spontaneous. They want to get rich; they want to earn passive income; they want to learn to invest and are ready to invest with their first pay cheque. Some of them understand that investments come with risks. They know that they might lose their money, but some of them ignore or underestimate the risks. They are willing to take the chance and risk their money. Even if they don't know how to budget, they use their hard-earned money to invest.

High-risk instruments will always give a high return. Low-risk instruments come with lower returns. High-risk instruments look attractive, and many people, especially young working adults, tend to look into maximising their returns because they assume that they have the time and want to invest in something that gives them the highest return. They fail to recognise the risk the instrument carries and do not consider the consequences if the market turns against them, which stands an equally high chance as the market being in their favour. This may result in them losing all their savings and money invested.

When you're looking into investments, especially high-risk instruments, always be mindful that there is a big chance of losing *everything*. Always consult with informed people before investing.

6.2.4 Time is never on our side

Many young people think time is on their side. They are young, they can do anything, and they can spend however they want with no concern for the future. Truth is, time is never on anyone's side, and it is not good to think that way. If you map out your life, you'll realise that there is never enough time, because there are many stages in your life that you have to work for. In fact, some may argue that time and life are too short! There's never enough around for you to do everything.

Stages in your life such as marriage and children (and their education) require hard work and money. When one life event ends, another follows, and there seems to be no end to it. For example, if you start working at 25 years old and plan to retire at 65, you'll be working for forty years of your life. Assuming you'll live to 90 years old, you're basically working forty years but having to save for a retirement fund that can last you twenty-five years. Are you confident that by the age of 65, you'll have enough money to enjoy your retirement?

The thing about young people is that they think they still have time before getting into saving for a long-term investment. But each time you delay, you'll have a shorter time for your money to accumulate.

6.2.5 Health never gets better

Another financial mistake people make is to think that their health will remain the same every year. In fact, your health is going to deteriorate every year, whether you like it or not. I was talking to a friend about how fast we used to run when we were in the air force: 2.4 kilometres in under 9 minutes 40 seconds. These days, running 2.4 kilometres takes 12 minutes. It is a fact that we grow older each day. Our mindset may stay young but not our health.

Some people continue to live a lavish life of partying and drinking even as they age. Nothing wrong with that, but such nightlife does pose a threat to the body, and you can't expect your health to not deteriorate. Many people think that their health is going to be constant for the rest of their life and tend to ignore risk management, such as getting medical insurance. They often wait until their body is showing symptoms before purchasing insurance, which will only become costlier.

Many people, not just the younger generation, do not see medical insurance as something important and feel that it is okay to not have any medical coverage. And many older people I have spoken to actually think it is bad luck to buy medical insurance. The thing is, medical insurance is just a small premium that you can afford which gives you coverage in the event that you are hospitalised. You do not have to worry if unfortunate events arise, and your medical costs won't be a financial burden upon you or your family.

6.3 Money habits for students

To structure their finances, secondary school students can first find out how much allowance they are getting and how much they can set aside for three different purposes: spending, saving, and donating to charity. It is simpler for younger people, because they can just divide their money between those three categories. This creates a basic habit for them to adopt, and as they grow up, they will start to understand budgeting and allocation, making it easier for them to save in the future.

One way parents can motivate and encourage teens to do this is to actually top up a dollar each time the teen saves a dollar. This will teach the idea of saving.

If teens want to donate to a certain cause, organisation, or campaign, ask them how much they are willing to donate. If they choose to donate an amount more than their allowance, or so much that they wouldn't have enough to spend on their meals, then you should stop them, because it would be an unwise decision. For them, it shouldn't be about the amount they put into these three categories but more about the habit of doing so and acquiring the strategy of properly allocating their money.

I have always believed that financial education starts young. When my child started getting an allowance for school at primary 1 (7 years old), I bought two piggy banks for him to drop his money in, one for savings and one for charity. Practicing what I teach, I dropped an additional coin into his piggy bank each time he saved.

6.4 Just started working

One of the biggest problems for young working adults is that the moment they are done with school and receive their first pay cheque, they realise they can now afford the many things they want to buy which they couldn't afford in the past with just an allowance from their parents. This is very dangerous, as they will start splurging on different things without budgeting first. This mainly includes lifestyle expenses. Their choice of food becomes more expensive, and the things they buy increase in quantity. However, they are unable to manage their money, resulting in either debt or lack of savings and emergency funds.

This is why I came up with the 60–10 rule—so young people know exactly how much money they should set aside to spend, save, and invest. Assuming people start working at the age of 20 and plan to retire at 65, they will spend about forty years of their life working. If they pass on at the age of 80 or 90, they will be working forty years of their life to support thirty years of retirement. A piece of advice for people who have just started working is to start saving for your retirement from the moment you start working. This ties down how you budget your money.

Another issue I have noticed among many young working adults is moving in and out of jobs or planning for a career transition. It's scary to lose a job—you have no idea whether you'll be able to get a job quickly or if your savings will be enough to sustain you and your family until that happens. Therefore, you need to be saving while you're currently working. How much should you save for it to be enough, or how much is needed during your career transition?

The Money Map provides practical goals to help you save efficiently as well as have enough money to enjoy right now. This will ensure that you save enough but not at the expense of having to live stingily today. Many young adults believe that they have a lot of time and can enjoy the present moment rather than saving for retirement later on in life. This is far from the truth. Financial planning should start from the moment you start working. This will form a saving or investing habit that can be inculcated over the years.

There are also people who are so obsessed with saving for retirement that they forget to leave much for today. Having just enough for the daily necessities is no way to live. The amount set aside to spend today should at least give you the luxury of choice to purchase what you want. Moreover, there is no point in saving for the future if you can't enjoy the present. If you follow the 60–10 rule, it is likely that you will be able to save a substantial amount for the future while enjoying the present.

6.5 People who are planning to raise a family

If you are in this group, map out the age of everyone in your household, including your children. For example, if you're 25 years old and married and you plan to have children by the age of 28, your financial map will show you how old you'll be when your oldest child enters primary 1 and how old your second or third child will be and so on—and what will be the plans for them. Next, think about when you turn 40; will your children be in primary school, secondary school, or pre-university? Will your child be entering university just when you want to retire? Will there be enough in your savings account to support them through university? If not, it might not be a prime time to retire.

The Money Map will show you an overview of the life of everyone in your family and the various milestones each of you will go through. It is important to map out the dreams you have through your whole life, as this will aid you in your financial goals. Your plan to retire at a certain age may disrupted due to your child's stage of life at that time. Financial mapping will provide you with a clearer view of events you will deal with at different ages.

6.6 Middle-aged professionals

When middle-aged professionals talk about value, their immediate thoughts will be asset value. If you have $10,000, who will you invest in? The correct answer is *you*. Invest in yourself.

One way to go is to set aside money to upgrade yourself. Many people tend to neglect this once they graduate from university. You may have heard the saying, "Learning is a lifelong journey." It is important to constantly upgrade yourself and add value to yourself, especially within your industry. There will always be certificates or courses catering to whatever you are doing in your industry.

If you are not interested in studying what your industry has to offer, find something else to up your value. It could be attending a photography class, a pottery class, or even a cooking or language class. These classes are fun and also increase your value as an individual. Focus on increasing your value first before investing in your asset.

In the course of my work, I met many famous and reputable people, including some who headed large organisations. When they were in power, people respected them because of their title. The true test of respect is how people treat you when you are not in power. Will people still show you the same amount of respect? I hear the flattering comments people make when you are in power, and when you are not, they do not even bother saying hello to you. I am sure you know what I mean; you have seen this many times.

As for me, I am flattered by the compliments I have received. I always evaluate the comments people make, and I am open to feedback (although, trust me, it is tough to listen to so many people's feedback). To me, feedback can be either subjective or objective. If it is subjective, it is just someone's personal view of a matter, so you should take it as a form of comment, since you cannot stop what people want to say. If it is objective feedback, you should take it seriously and see how you can improve from it. Often, the feedback comes because you did not communicate well, and people did not understand your intentions.

There are just too many opportunities in the marketplace. You do not need to invest in everything people offer, even if it is the best deal in the world. This is what I always live by. Warren Buffett advised that you should "never invest in a business you cannot understand." I have received lots of calls and emails from people looking to offer me opportunities in businesses and investments; they will learn that I do not invest in things that I am not sure of. I am always happy to refer another contact of mine if I think that can help them succeed.

After investing in yourself, the next step is to allocate your money into an asset. For a middle-aged professional, after managing cash flow, there will be a surplus every month. This surplus can be allocated into an asset that will bring an income in the future. This is passive income that contributes a cash flow back into your savings. Later, I will touch on how to allocate money properly, be it for a higher-risk instrument or a lower risk instrument.

6.7 Retiring soon

Clients approaching retirement were the ones I met with the most when I was working in the local bank. Their only regret was that they hadn't started saving and investing earlier. They hoped to clear their loans so that they could retire with peace of mind.

To structure your Money Map, the first thing to start on is always your cash flow. It is crucial to know how to manage your cash flow properly and to understand the financial dreams you will face in the next five to ten years. This could include a goal to retire in fifteen years' time, but you also might intend to buy another property in five years' time. This will definitely have an effect on your retirement funds, and that has to be taken into consideration.

Start on the cash flow first; after that, you can look at the financial map and identify the goals you have for the next 5 to 10 years. Lastly, look at how you can structure your assets and liabilities properly. If you're moving towards retirement, try to reduce your liabilities while increasing the value of your assets. For people who are retiring, another major part is managing their risks as well, such as planning where and how they allocate their money so as to face minimal risk while getting maximum returns.

7

BEING HONEST WITH YOUR CRYSTAL BALL

The first step to having the money to take advantage of current opportunities is to be honest with yourself about your spending. Many people struggle with this. It could be due to the fact that they don't know how to track their spending, or they might be ashamed of their spending and how much they actually spend. This deters them from being honest when it comes to utilising the Money Map concept.

The second step is to be honest about your financial goals and what you want to achieve in the next five to ten years. Even though I haven't encountered many problems with adults being honest in this area, I've still met people, young adults especially, who are lost and unsure about their plans for the future. They do not know what to expect and do not have foresight for their lives. This is pretty common, given how similar I was to them in the past. However, I realised that it wasn't very wise to wander around and not think about the future and keep thinking that you're still very young—too young to plan for your future.

7.1 Planning for the Future

There is no such thing as being too young to plan for your future. It is better to start planning as soon as possible. If you're still unsure about your future, it is best to think about it, or list the things that you wish to do in the future. From there, you can gauge and utilise this simple concept to the fullest.

To assess and monitor your future plans, there are two things to take note of. Firstly, the Money Map concept assesses the risk an individual is willing to take, because the market can be volatile. Some people enjoy the volatility, whereas others might be more conservative.

This concept will help to draft a financial map for you. It will show how the financial plan matches with the risk-return and the volatility of the market they are in. For example, a client wanted to move to a new house in three years' time and asked if it would be an appropriate time to do so. We decided to map it out.

Upon doing so, we realised that in three years' time, her child would be entering primary 1. I asked if the property she was planning to buy was an investment property or just so that her family could move nearer to her child's school. This was an important difference: if the property was meant to be an investment, the location should be a key factor. If the property was meant for the child to be near the school, it would not be considered an investment property.

Back in my banking days, I got to meet and deal with high-net-worth individuals. There was one instance where I met a guy called Mr Teo. He was my client, and I remember that he was working as an engineer. Mr Teo was a very systematic person. It was during one of our appointments that he asked me a very random question: "Where are you staying?"

I told him I had gotten a flat in an area slightly outside Singapore's central business district. When I bought the flat, it cost me $250,000. When he asked about the current market value, I told him it was about $700,000.

He asked me what I would do with this property. I was surprised by the question and asked him why he was asking me that. My plan was to stay in this property and continue to save money until I could buy a second one to rent out. Mr Teo asked if this was what everybody my age thought, and I told him yes, as it made the most sense, practically speaking.

7.2 Resetting the game

As I was writing this book, coronavirus, or COVID-19, was becoming a regional and then a worldwide pandemic, causing many countries to go on lockdown. Businesses and jobs were affected, with most countries imposing travel restrictions. The number of tourists decreased, and this had a negative impact on businesses. Sales dropped as a result of this, and employees were asked to take no-pay leaves.

The stock market had the biggest one-day drop in decades. Millions of people were on the verge of losing their jobs or wealth overnight. Companies couldn't operate because of the lockdown, and goods and services were affected.

With all of that, I had never been so excited to be working in the finance industry. While some people lost their wealth, there were others, usually not reported, who made a fortune from the stock market or the services they provided because of the pandemic. One of my clients who owns a cleaning company had increased his business over this period, and he took the opportunity to widen his market shares and increase awareness of his services. Meanwhile, another friend who had been doing very well before the crisis was losing hundreds of thousands of dollars.

You were undoubtedly affected by this virus too. While there are losses in a crisis, there are also opportunities. My book was completed during this period while I was stuck at home. The idea of a mobile application and a board game called Money CEO also came about because I had so much more free time to think.

This was a period in which people made and lost money dramatically. It was much like playing board games. If there was a ranking table of everyone's wealth, some people moved up and some moved down. Some had a total reset to their game. Whatever it was, it was like a reset of the game now. Think about it: if there was no crisis, there was no way to move up the ranking table of wealth and beat the guy in front of you.

A crisis also means lots of opportunity in the market. I am not talking about cheap and discounted equities only, but a discount in almost every asset class. Some businesses closed due to cash flow issues, and this was an opportunity for those who had money on hand. What was most important was whether or not you had the money to take advantage of the opportunity.

8

BEYOND THAT PENCIL

Earning money is great. Earning a lot is even greater, and being rich is awesome. Have you ever met a very rich but sad man? It's ironic, isn't it? One can own everything in this world but lose one's health, one's marriage, and one's future. Let's imagine a world where there's a limit to everyone's net profit, and you've reached the maximum amount. How can you go beyond that 100 per cent? How can you earn more when you're already at the maximum? How do you get that hundred and *one*?

At this point, if you still think we're talking about money, I'm sorry to disappoint. The *one* stands for the many things that make the hundred worthwhile. I'm talking about things that are beyond monetary value—things like your health, your happiness, and your future. These should be more valuable than money but have sometimes, or even most of the time, been sacrificed to obtain more money.

Many people think that money can bring them happiness. Well, technically, it can, and it will probably bring you to a maximum of 100 per cent happiness. The extra *one* we are talking about here cannot be bought with any amount of money. It is priceless. It is something that many rich people with that 100 per cent maximised wealth wish they had.

I've met and known people who have obtained that 100 per cent wealth and are very rich, but they are unhappy, lonely, or struggling with their health. The purpose of publishing this book is to help you understand that health and happiness are equally as important as money. I want to help you achieve that overflow, to have a balance between being wealthy and being healthy. After all, what's the point of being rich and having a lot of money if you are not healthy enough to live long enough to be able to spend it wisely?

When you're wealthy and healthy, you can give back to society. You can share your stories and experiences with others, and help them to gain the hundred and *one*.

Epilogue

The whole journey of money mapping, monitoring your cash flow, and even budgeting is not easy. It takes time to develop this habit. It takes effort to be consistent and to be disciplined with your money. I've been through that; I've had trouble keeping my money together. I've met people who can't seem to budget no matter how hard they try. Some even landed themselves heavily in debt, feeling unhappy all the time, unsure whether there was a way out.

That's why I've created this concept called the Money Map. I believe that once you understand cash flow and have seen your personal cash flow, you'll be able to start saving or investing effectively. I hope this book gave you an insight into how to be good a money manager and also how you can find ways to constantly make money work for you. With this knowledge that I've garnered through my years in the financial industry, I truly believe everyone can be millionaires or billionaires. Let's change our mindsets today and start working toward our dream in a smart way.

Ultimately, I hope that by writing this book and launching my very own Money Map concept, I will help people who can't seem to get everything together, as well as people who wonder why their money is never enough. I want to help these people sort out their finances—to gain a bird's-eye view and clarity. Many people are actually rich if only they knew how to manage their money. I wish you all the best, and I hope you'll get your pencil soon.

Appendix

MONEY TIPS FROM MY STUDENTS

I will share here some money tips from my successful students. I would like to thank them for their contributions and for sharing their experiences with everyone.

Tip 1: "You need to plan!" Alastair Chan

■ ALASTAIR CHAN

Finance, like gardening, requires a plan first. Until we start planning and putting the plan into action, there will be no trees or fruits in the future to shade us from the sun, to build a swing to swing our children from, and to provide food for us.

Everyone knows that it is important to plan. However, the other important aspect is to take the required action to make sure that we apply what we have planned and review it along the journey. Reviewing our financial plans is like caring for the seeds we have planted. We must water them, rid them of weeds, and provide care.

Like every other thing in life, our plans and priorities will determine where we end up. If we show a bit more care, and put time and effort into our financial plans, the trees will eventually bear fruit. Just as the seed requires time to grow, so do our financial plans. It may seem daunting, as the questions we have to answer are tough to predict. But if you plan it, apply it, and review it, you will watch it bear the fruits you so wish for.

Tip 2: "Let your money work for you." Benjamin Ng

BENJAMIN NG

We all have dreams. We have stuff we want to buy, events we want to experience, and goals we hope to achieve. We've got our current financial responsibilities, such as dining, entertainment, or buying clothes to look good. We've also got long-term goals like retirement, homes, and cars (note the plural), and if you're like me, sharing experiences as often as possible with family and friends.

Most of us have a finite amount of money, and that's where the problem lies if we don't prioritise. I've gone through numerous financial roller coasters, and here are the three key lessons I've taken away:

1. **Learn to invest in yourself.** I am passionate about investment, and I share it with all my clients because it makes money work harder for them. I have noticed that people fear investment because of the uncertainty that comes along with them, but what if I told you there was an investment that gave you a huge and guaranteed return? How much would you be willing to put in? This unbelievable investment you can make is in *you*. There are so many ways to invest in yourself and experience exponential growth in your life. Read more. Find a mentor. Insure yourself. Create a passive income. Take a break. Learn to say no. Boss your money.

2. **Learn to spend within your means.** You are the boss of your money. As much as it is tempting to get the latest gadget or the hottest outfit, do not get it if it puts you in debt. Do not dress to impress others if it puts you in debt. Debt is no fun, and it pulls you down. There are debts that are inevitable, such as housing or student loans, but your money is not truly yours until you are debt-free. We are stewards over our money, and we need wisdom in managing our cash flow. James Chen taught me a valuable lesson that as much as it is important to track my expenses, it is better to manage my cash flow.
3. **Let your money work for you**. If there's one thing I wish I had done earlier, it would be to invest. A key reason I joined this industry was because I wanted to generate more wealth for my family and friends, to use money to love people. Investment need not be scary if done correctly. Use time to your advantage and let compounding interest and your money work hard for you. Engage a professional, but do not be pressured to take on a risk you are uncomfortable with. Always ask questions when in doubt. Remember that it is your money, and you are the boss.

In conclusion, I pray that my lessons and experiences will help you to not make the mistakes I did.

Tip 3: "Start small, grow big." Bryaan Lea

▎BRYAAN LEA

Dedicate a fixed amount to a "set aside" account. For example, you can set a target for yourself to save $10 a day for the next thirty days.

Saving is a lifestyle, a habit. It is not easy to save when there are always so many things to buy. In fact, research has shown that habits take twenty-eight days to develop. Start small by saving $10 a day consistently for the next thirty days, and you're good to go with a new savings habit.

Investing may seem daunting, but if you meet the right financial advisor, it is the best way to grow your wealth. Spending money or leaving it in a bank is such a waste. Have your money work for you, and you'll be off to a good financial start.

Tip 4: "Every dollar makes a difference." CK Seah

▍C. K. Seah

Tend to your daily living expenses as you'd tend to your own business. You'd always want a positive cash flow for your company. It should be the same for your daily life. Ensure that you are always in positive cash flow in case of emergency. As you spend 60 per cent? You should use 40 per cent of your cash flow to invest into an instrument within your level of comfort to ensure growth of your wealth. Just as you'd want to grow the profits of a company through various investments, it should be that way for your life too.

Tip 5: "Invest in your greatest asset." Diana Koordi

Diana Koordi

One of the best investments you can make is to invest in yourself. Most millennials understand the importance of saving and investing our money. But not many people understand the importance of investing in yourself. Rarely do people spend time reading books or upgrading themselves.

Set a goal this year to put 5 to 10 per cent of your salary each month into an education fund for yourself. Alternatively, you can also utilise your SkillsFuture Credits (for Singaporeans) to take a subsidised course to improve yourself.

However, remember to choose wisely. Choose a course that can potentially give you a good return on investment. Don't waste your money on learning a new hobby that cannot generate returns.

> *Don't wish it was easier, wish you were better. Don't wish for less problems, wish for more skills. Don't wish for less challenge, wish for more wisdom.—Jim Rohn*

Tip 6: "Be a blessing." Freda Chua

▎Freda Chua

Nothing beats being in a position to bless another person. Money can be earned, and wealth can be accumulated. But one thing that adds true riches is to be of help to people who need it the most.

Giving back to the community can be done in any form or fashion, including sponsoring a child in need of an education, giving money to a cause you stand for, or volunteering your time for a non-profit organisation. The meaningful work you do not only benefits the beneficiary but also develops in you a sense of compassion and gratitude, while giving value to your time and money. It makes you a happy and cheerful giver.

As the saying goes, it's better to give than to receive. Kindness begets kindness.

Tip 7: "Start saving for retirement when you start working." Gaius Ng

▌ GAIUS NG

At a family gathering, I caught up with an uncle who had just retired. He revealed that he could retire with a comfortable lifestyle solely on the interest from his retirement fund. I was impressed.

When I asked about his contingency plans, especially when he needed to draw a lump sum out, he shared about his insurance coverage. Because he was covered for his critical illness and hospitalization needs, he did not need to dip into his retirement fund when unforeseen events happened. He knew that his plans would not be derailed and the funds would not be used for anything other than their intended purpose. What impressed me more was when I found out that he had started planning this when he started work!

Don't let your money idle, make it work for you.

Tip 8: "Map out before your money gets wiped out." Grace Kho

▍Grace Kho

Map out your life and gauge which stage is more financially needful. Many people are afraid to map out their lives, as they think that there isn't a point of it and the future is unpredictable. I used to think that way too. However, when I first mapped out my life, by having a brief gauge as to all the highlights of my life, such as marriage and child planning, I realised how important it was to consider all the different stages of life in the future and save accordingly.

These gauges will show you at which point of life you will require a hefty sum of money. This allows you to choose the right instrument for investment, as you're able to choose instruments which will mature when you need them.

Tip 9: "Investment is important for the young and the young at heart." Ivy Ho

▌ Ivy Ho

It is not about how much you earn, it is about how much you retain. Many young adults in Singapore have good earnings, but they let the money pass through their hands without retaining their wealth. Cash flow management is the key to ensuring that one spends within capacity. It involves making plans for meaningful saving and spending with good budgeting.

One of the social concerns in Singapore is longevity, and yet we may not have enough to sustain and maintain our lifestyle with a healthy financial status later in life. Is it fair that we save 30₵ for the future self for every $1 earned? Savings are not for a rainy day; savings empowers you to have the choice to invest when the time comes, growing your 30₵ to $1 in a reasonable time frame. The snowball effect and compounding growth are exponential.

One may think that savings can always be delayed; it is still early, so it is OK to opt for personal indulgences. Enjoyment and lifestyle may be the first priority of many who are in their twenties. What's next—saving when one turns 30? If people can't have proper saving habits in their twenties, what makes them think they can start doing so in their thirties? This is the life stage where one is likely to have higher expenses and liabilities. It is a stage of first property acquisition, marriage, babies, expensive hobbies, and so on.

In their forties, people start to realise the importance of savings. But many in their forties have more liabilities than those in their thirties—education fees, lifestyle upgrade, social status in life, and ageing parents who may require medical care and attention. Due to the low birth rate in Singapore, which is another social issue, the younger ones have to support two or more elderly parents, aunts, uncles, or even grandparents (remember the first social issue, longevity?), and some social responsibility for those elderly who have no family members to rely on. The true fact is many in their forties are unwilling to adjust their comfortable lifestyle. What happens when they enters their fifties? their sixties?

Granted, a healthy financial status doesn't guarantee a happy retirement, but with it, many problems can be solved easily. Do you want to enjoy your retirement life, or do you prefer to retire from your enjoyment? Do not underestimate the small steps. Start from saving 10₵ from every $1 earned, then increase it to 20₵, and eventually 30₵ or more. Get your first $100, first $1,000 to begin an investment, and begin your journey in wealth accumulation. Invest while accumulating your pot of gold. With the right objective and strategy, investment vehicles suited to your risk profile, and a reasonable time horizon, a comfortable future is definite.

Tip 10: "Discipline your spending." Jasmin Loh

▌ JASMIN LOH

When you're shopping online, add your desired items to the wish list instead of the shopping cart. If you're buying things online, chances are you do not need those items immediately. Stop buying things impulsively. That extra step of transferring your items from the wish list to your shopping cart buys you time to think, filter, and review your shopping list.

Make a conscious decision and think twice about whether you really need an item before purchasing it. Consolidate and check out only once a month. This way, you cultivate good spending habits by browsing and not buying every single time you see something you like.

Tip 11: "Save on costs." Jason Boon

▌Jason Boon

Dining can be a hefty part of your monthly expenses. In a food paradise like Singapore, it is important to plan your budgeting by recording your expenditures.

Look at where you spend and see how you can cut down on unnecessary spending. There are plenty of ways to dine at a fraction of the cost—for example, deals on the mobile application the Entertainer and apps that allow you to buy leftover food from restaurants at a fraction of the cost. Another app that I would recommend is Eatigo, which provides discounts for many restaurants. However, beware of overusing these apps to get your money's worth. You may end up spending much more.

During festive periods, it is likely that you will spend more eating out. It might be a good idea to go easy on your dining budget in the months leading up to Christmas, Chinese New Year, or Valentine's Day. Then you can dine without feeling guilty during those festive times.

By taking note of your expenditures, you can better plan your next goal, whether it is a family holiday, buying your dream home, or setting aside 20 per cent of your income for savings and investments. A little change will make a huge difference to your lifestyle.

Tip 12: "Future money is not your money." Kelvin Kek

Kelvin Kek

Do not count on "future" money, because it is not your money! When I was young, I thought that having many credit cards in my wallet would look nice and show that I was rich. I was under the impression that only people who are rich could apply for credit cards. However, I was totally wrong. My definition of *rich* was when I was able to spend money to buy the things I wanted and eat at dine-in restaurants. The reverse of this is that I became poor before the month of my next pay cheque because I would have to pay back what I had spent on my cards.

I thought that if I signed and paid in full, I would be fine. But again, I was wrong, because most of my salary went into making credit card payments, and I was left with no savings in the bank. With no savings, I had to rely on credit cards for payment towards the end of the month, and not only did this happen once or twice, it continued for many months. Then, the debts start to roll over and become bigger and bigger; along with the high credit-card interest rate charged by the banks (which are basically like legal loan sharks that haunt you towards the end of every month if you miss any payment and add late charges to your account. Don't think that the banks are nice!).

This not only caused stress to myself but also to my family and the people around me. I have learned my lesson, and with help from my family, I have slowly cleared my credit card debt.

Tip 13: "Start now to invest in yourself." Michelle Tok

▌Michelle Tok

Start tracking your expenses for the next thirty days. Identify your biggest expense and make a conscious attempt to reduce this expense by 20 per cent. Save and invest this amount to better cope with your expenses.

Tracking your expenses is very important. You have to identify the biggest pocket-burner before you can plan your savings. There are many spending tracking apps out there which are user-friendly and help you identify your largest expense. Once you are able to identify it and reduce that expense, you will be able to use the savings to grow more savings so that eventually, your expenses will be exceeded by the passive income that you earn through investing.

Tip 14: "It is never too early to manage your own finances." Pei Xuan

▍Pei Xuan

Start to develop an interest in managing your own finances at a young age, even before you start working officially as an adult. Most people only start to worry about how they should plan and manage their finances after they start working. That is when the reality of not receiving any more pocket money and having to work for a salary to pay for bills and daily expenses hits most of us. Many young adults age 24 and below don't see the need to plan for their finances in detail and don't commit to doing so because of the "It's still early, I'm still young" mindset. However, when reality hits and they realise that they have to start budgeting but don't actually know how, they might find themselves panicking.

Thus, it is important to start planning and managing your personal finances in the early stages of your life so that when the time comes, you won't be struggling to save enough and have enough to spend at the same time. Even if you don't start managing your own finances directly before you start working as an adult, it is important to at least develop an interest in doing so and find out the different ways of managing your own finances effectively. With that interest developed, you will have so much more information and knowledge on financial planning and management that you won't be so lost when the time comes.

Unfortunately, you have come to the end of this book. But fret not: this is not the end of our journey together. This is merely the beginning!

In order for us to continue on this fulfilling journey together, I have created a mobile application and attached a full Money Map worksheet. Money CEO, the mobile application, is available for download on both Apple's App Store and Android's Play Store.

To find out more about Money Map and the Money CEO, visit www.jameschen.sg.

If you're curious about how Money Map works and want to know more in detail, please get in touch with me and I'll be happy to share.

MONEY MAP™

Prepared for: _____   Prepared by: _____   Date: _____

DOB: _____

DOB: _____

DOB: _____

DOB: _____

DOB: _____

DOB: _____

DOB: _____

LEGEND

Maturity of asset	A	Getting a house	H	Retirement	R
Having a baby	B	Getting a job	J	Travel & fun	T
Getting a car	C	Loan	L		
Death of loved one	D	Getting married	M		

MONEY MAP™

ASSETS

-
-

Property :
Vehicle :
Cash Savings:
CPF OA :
CPF SA :
CPF MA :
Others: :
Others: :

Total Assets :

Net Position :

LIABILITIES

-
-

Housing Loan :
Car Loan :
Study Loan :
Personal Loan :
Others: :
Others: :

Total Liabilities :

RISK MANAGEMENT

CASHFLOW

(+) INCOME

Monthly Gross Income :
Other Income :
CPF Contribution :
Bonus (No. of months) :
Others: :
Total Home Income :

(-) MONTHLY EXPENSES

Dining Out / Entertainment :
Shopping / Hobbies :
Insurance / Investment :
Transports :
Loan Repayment (Cash) :
Others: :
Total Expenses :

Net Position :

ALLOCATION

Remarks:
- P__Y____
- T__A____
- P____L___
- W____I___

Prepared for: _____ Prepared by: _____ Date: _____

www.ingramcontent.com/pod-product-compliance
Lightning Source LLC
Chambersburg PA
CBHW030916180526
45163CB00004B/1849